Robot world

CONTENTS

Introduction

Robots are machines that do jobs for people. In stories robots do amazing things. This book will tell you what robots in real life *can* do . . .

and *cannot* do . . .

Robots in stories and films often look and think like people. When they move, their metal arms and legs jerk. Their heads turn on stiff necks.

In real life, robots are not shaped like people. They cannot think and must always be told what to do. A real robot is often just a **mechanical** arm and hand.

Most robot arms are fixed in one place.
Sometimes they move around on **buggies**.

Programming robots

This robot arm is programmed to butter toast.

A robot is worked by computer. The computer is **programmed** with instructions. The instructions tell the robot when and how to move. A video recorder is programmed to switch on and off in just the same way.

A video recorder is programmed to switch on and off.

Different kinds of robot

There are lots of different kinds of robot. They can do all kinds of different things. There are robots which can . . .

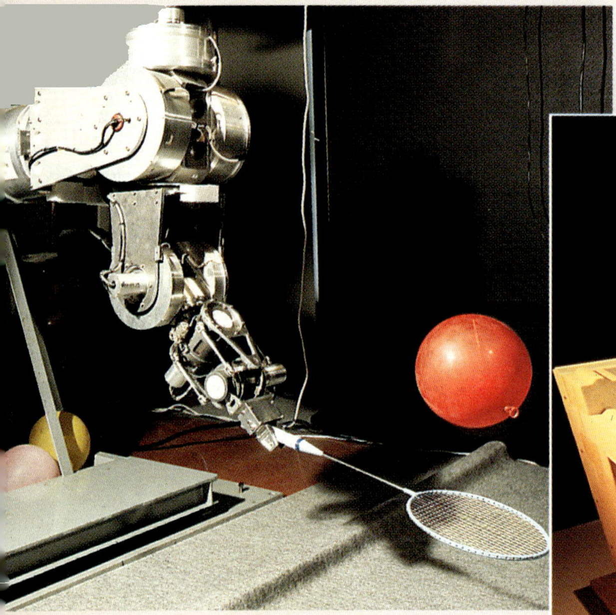

. . . bat a balloon

. . . build a model house

. . . dig a hole

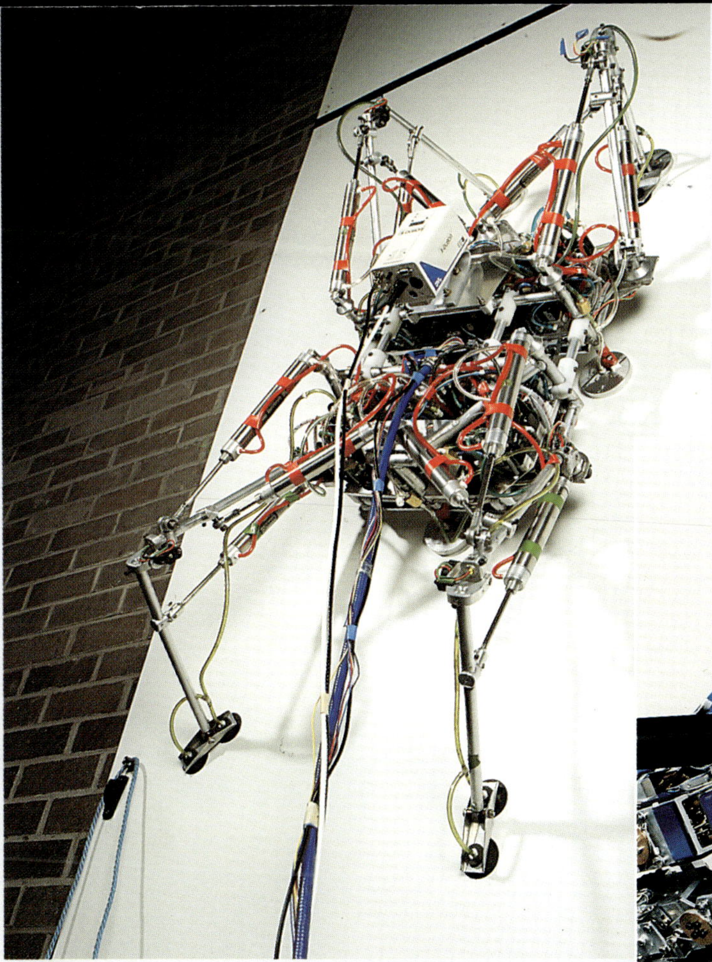

. . . climb a wall

. . . write in Japanese

. . . make clothes

. . . or even play chess.

Factory robots

Robots in factories do the same jobs over and over again. Thousands of robot arms work in factories all over the world.

School robots

Simple robots are used in some schools. Children learn to program the robot's computer. They can make the robot move around an obstacle course.

Remote control robots

Remote control robots are programmed by radio. A person works the robot from a distance. This is like working a radio-controlled model car.

Remote control robots can be sent into dangerous places. Robots on buggies put out fires. Robots with **video cameras** inspect bombs.

Space robots

The Viking probe was a remote control robot.

It was sent to **Mars** by rocket.

Viking landed on Mars. Scientists on Earth worked the robot arm by radio.

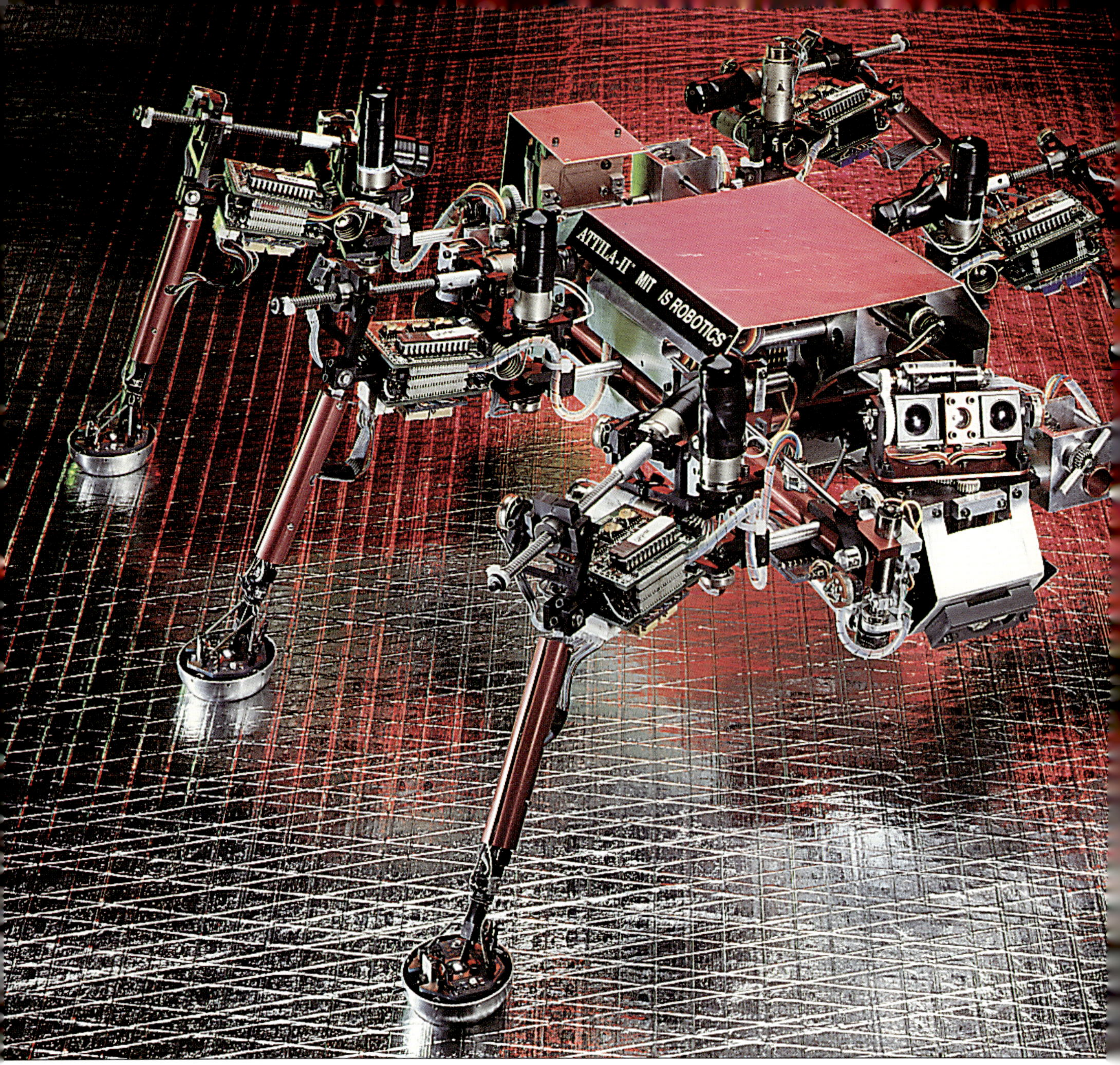

Experimental robots

Scientists are trying to build robots which can do more difficult jobs. This robot insect was built by American scientists. It can find its own way around a room. It learns to move around obstacles.

The robot insect has **sensors** to stop it bumping into things. Sensors are electric eyes, ears and feelers. They are linked to the robot's computer brain.

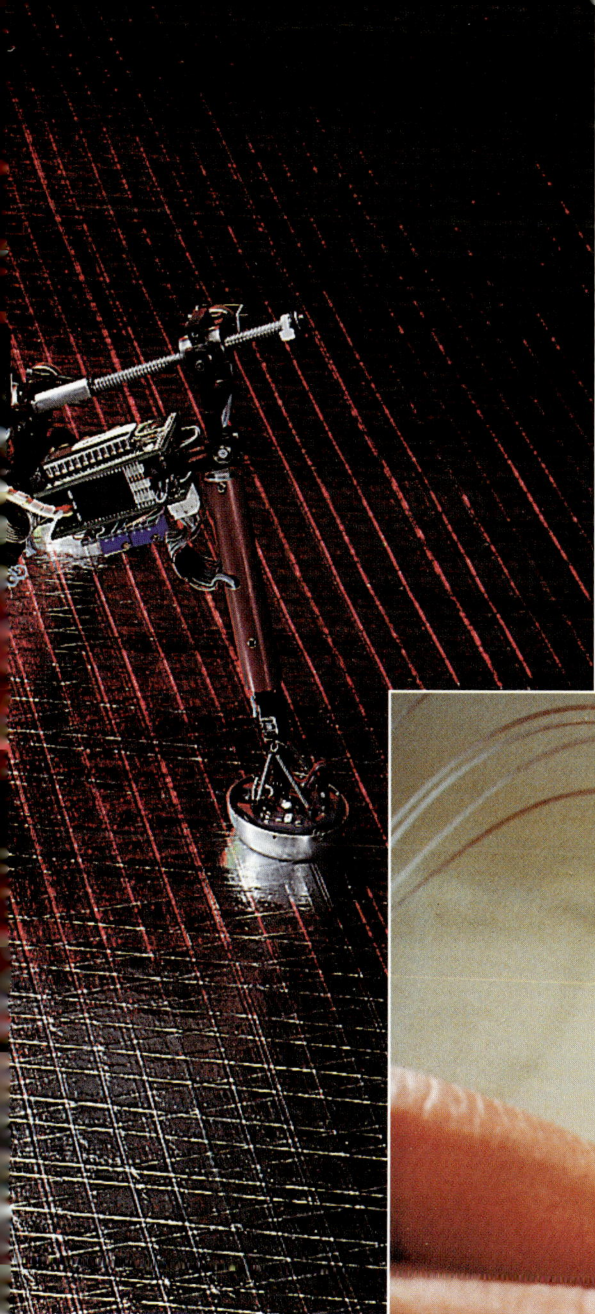

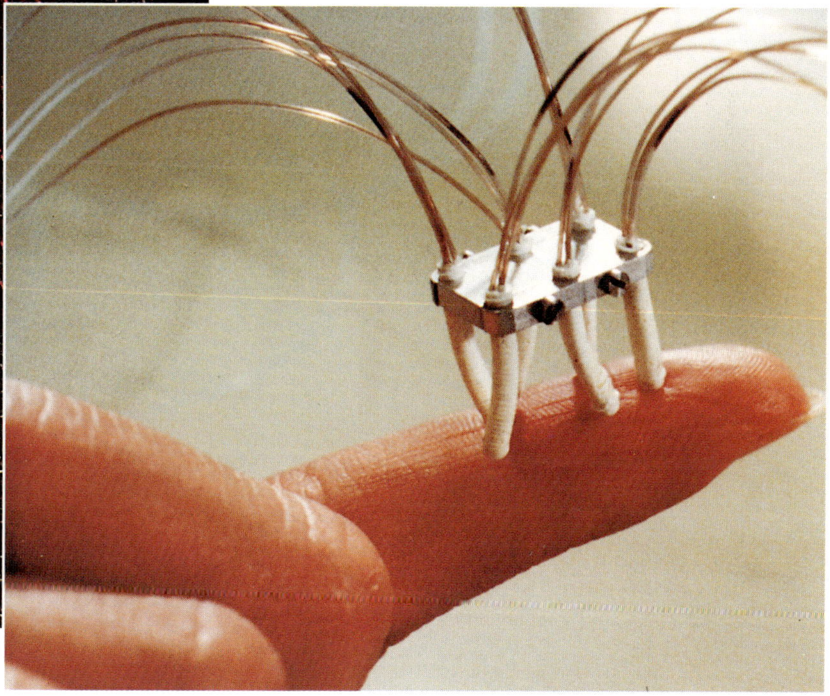

This tiny robot is small enough to walk on a finger.

Robot future

In the future there will be many more robots. Scientists are experimenting with robot vehicles. A robot vehicle could find the fastest way between two places. Sensors would stop it crashing into things.

Who knows what robots will do in the future? Some people think we might have robots to cook and clean . . .

. . . robot pets

. . . even robot teachers!

Index